GREEN TECH

SOLVING THE CLIMATE CRISIS

ALICE HARMAN

PowerKiDS press

New York

Published in 2023 by The Rosen Publishing Group, Inc.
29 East 21st Street, New York, NY 10010

Series Editor: Alice Harman
Series Designer: Rocket Design (East Anglia) Ltd
Consultant: Dr Sharon George

Cataloging-in-Publication Data

Names: Harman, Alice.
Title: Solving the climate crisis / Alice Harman.
Description: New York : Powerkids Press, 2023. | Series: Green tech | Includes glossary and index.
Identifiers: ISBN 9781725338692 (pbk.) | ISBN 9781725338715 (library bound) | ISBN 9781725338708 (6pack) | ISBN 9781725338722 (ebook)
Subjects: LCSH: Climatic changes--Juvenile literature. | Climate change mitigation--Juvenile literature.| Environmentalism--Juvenile literature.
Classification: LCC QC903.H37 2023 | DDC 363.738'74--dc23

Picture acknowledgements:
Shutterstock: Suesig cover tl, Boyko.Pictures cover tr, bl, br and 1, Jack1e cover ml and bc, Roi and Roi cover mc and 1, B illustrations cover mr and 1, all_is_magic 2 and 14, Nadiinko 3, 30 and 32 icons, davooda 4 and 31 icons, VectorMine 4 and 31, Piyaset 5t, elenabsl 5b, 7 and 30, petovarga 6, Puchong Art 6 icon, SIHASAKPRACHUM 8, graphic stocker 8 icon, PI 9t, sahua d 9b, VectorV 10 icon, TebNad 11, sivVector 12, Suchat Siriboot 12 inset, sadedesign 12 icon, OxfordSquare 13t, Novikov Aleksey 13b, T VECTOR ICONS 14 icon, iacomino FRiMAGES 15t, Alejo Miranda 15b, aapsky 16, Abstract man 24 16 icon, OSORIOartist 17, tofutyklein 18 inset, UI 18 icon, Viktor Chursin 19t, AlexHliv 19t, Jackie Niam 19b, phipatbig 19b, ProStockStudio 19b and 32, Uncle Leo 20t, Alexandre Laprise 20m, Lilkin 21, Marccophoto 22tl, Kent Weakley 22tr, VectorPlotnikoff 22b, Nova II 22 icon, Visual Generation 23, MarcelClemens 24, VoodooDot 24 icon, graphicwithart 25t, bygermina 26, nexusby 26 icon, Molesko Studio 28b, artyway 28 icon, Joost van Uffelen 29.

All design elements from Shutterstock or drawn by designer.

Manufactured in the United States of America

CPSIA Compliance Information: Batch #CSPK23. For further information contact Rosen Publishing, New York, New York at 1-800-237-9932.

CONTENTS

WHAT IS THE CLIMATE CRISIS?	4
ELECTRIC AND HYBRID CARS	6
HIGH-SPEED TRAINS	8
WIND POWER	10
SOLAR POWER	12
GEOTHERMAL ENERGY AND GROUND SOURCE HEAT	14
USING SATELLITES	16
EXTRACTING ICE CORES	18
LAB-GROWN MEAT	20
CLIMATE-RESISTANT CROPS	22
SOLAR GEOENGINEERING	24
CARBON CAPTURE AND STORAGE	26
REFORESTATION AND REWILDING	28
GLOSSARY	30
FURTHER INFORMATION	31
INDEX	32

WHAT IS THE CLIMATE CRISIS?

To understand what the climate crisis is, let's look at how things should be working with Earth's climate—and how humans have caused major problems by upsetting its natural balance.

THE GREENHOUSE EFFECT

As far as we know, Earth is the only liveable planet in our solar system. It's close enough to the sun to be warm, but not so close that it gets too hot. It's also surrounded by an invisible atmosphere made of different gases, some of which stop the sun's heat from completely escaping back out into space. This is what we call "the greenhouse effect."

Without heat-trapping greenhouse gases, such as carbon dioxide and methane, Earth would get too cold. However, over the last 200 years, human activities—such as chopping down forests and burning fossil fuels (coal, gas, and oil)—have released a huge amount of these gases. Too much of the sun's heat is getting trapped, and Earth is getting too hot. We call this "global warming."

CLIMATE CHANGE

Earth's rising temperature is throwing our planet's complicated natural systems out of balance, causing what we call "climate change," or Earth's "climate crisis." Hot, dry areas are getting even hotter and drier, and suffering more droughts and forest fires. Wetter areas are flooding more often because of heavier rain and storms.

WHAT CAN WE DO?

To stop Earth from becoming unliveably hot and dangerous, we need to massively cut our greenhouse gas emissions. Luckily, there are a variety of amazing green technologies that can help us do this! We also need to put in lots of effort to make eco-friendly choices in our own lives and push governments and businesses to make large-scale changes.

DID YOU KNOW?

Climate change is about long-term changes, not day-to-day weather. Even though Earth's temperature is rising, we still get cold weather sometimes.

ELECTRIC AND HYBRID CARS

Most cars are powered by engines that burn gasoline or diesel fuel made from crude oil, a fossil fuel pumped out from deep underground. Burning these fuels releases greenhouse gases and other types of air pollution, seriously harming the planet and people's health. Luckily, there's a much cleaner, greener alternative: electric cars.

Electric cars are powered by rechargeable batteries. Instead of refilling the car's fuel tank, the driver charges the batteries.

CLEANER AND GREENER

Electric cars don't burn any liquid fuel, so they don't release greenhouse gases or other air pollution as they drive along. Hybrid cars are powered partly by electricity and partly by gas or diesel, switching between the two systems. They give off far fewer emissions than traditional cars but more than purely electric cars.

DID YOU KNOW?

Back in 1900, around a third of all road vehicles in the US were powered by electricity. However, cheaper gas-powered cars soon became much more popular.

ELECTRIC CARS FOR EVERYONE?

So what's stopping everyone from buying electric cars? Firstly, the cost; they are typically still more expensive than traditional cars. Secondly, many countries don't yet have enough charging stations for drivers to use on long journeys.

Many people like hybrid cars because they're a cheaper eco-friendly option, and they can be refueled at gas stations. Some hybrid cars don't ever need to be plugged into charging stations because they recharge their batteries as they go by capturing energy from the car's movement.

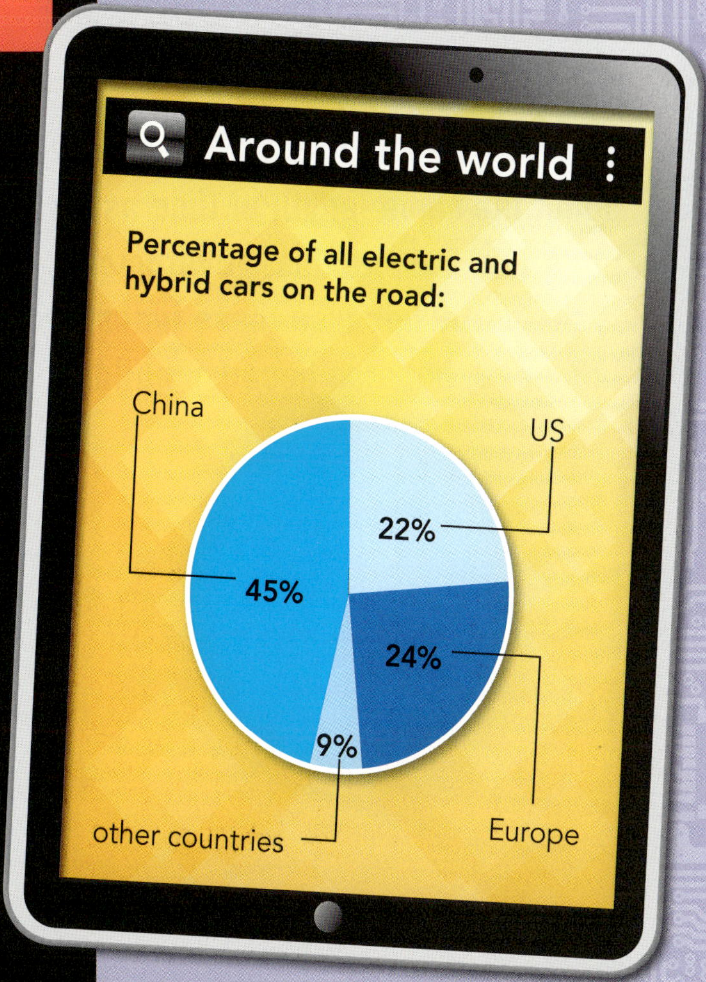

ECO-FRIENDLY ELECTRICITY

It's important that the electricity used to charge up cars comes from eco-friendly sources. If it is generated by power plants burning coal or other fossil fuels, harmful emissions are still created. Instead, we need to use non-polluting energy sources, such as wind and solar power (see pages 10–13).

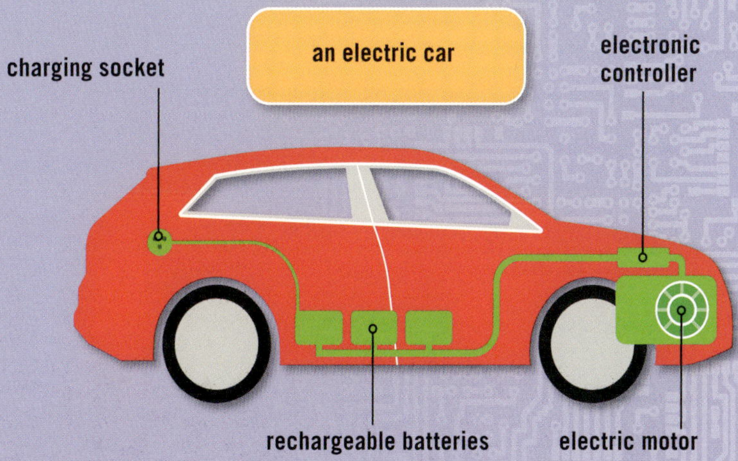

HIGH-SPEED TRAINS

Traveling on a high-speed train powered by clean electricity can take about the same length of time as an airplane flight while causing far less pollution. Despite this, governments often put air and road travel projects first—partly because these industries have so much money and political influence, but also because building new high-speed tracks is expensive.

TRAINS AND TRACKS

High-speed train systems are specially designed to safely go much faster than ordinary trains. The trains have smooth, curved shapes to help them push through air more easily. They are typically powered by overhead electric wires, which they connect to through a raised "arm" called a pantograph.

First and fastest

First high-speed rail system: The Shinkansen "bullet train," Japan (1964) – 130 miles per hour (210 kph)

Fastest high-speed train in operation: Shanghai maglev, China – 268 mph (431 kph)

Fastest high-speed train in development: Lo Series, Japan – 375 mph (603 kph)

a tunnel-boring machine

TERRIFIC TUNNELS

Tunnels allow high-speed trains to race through mountainous areas and under the sea. Huge tunnel-boring machines (TBMs) use a spinning plate covered with cutters to drill through rock. TBMs are usually powered by polluting diesel fuel, so we have to consider this against the benefits of new train routes.

Underwater tunnels can be built using the "cut and cover" method. Workers dig a trench in the ocean floor and sink steel or concrete tubes into it, then connect these tubes to form tunnels and cover them with rock.

MAGLEV MAGIC

The latest high-speed train technology is maglev—short for "magnetic levitation." Rather than running on wheels along traditional railway lines, maglev trains float just above special tracks fitted with strong magnets that hold them safely in place. Because they don't make contact with the track, there is no friction (rubbing) to slow them down and they can run more safely at higher speeds than wheeled trains.

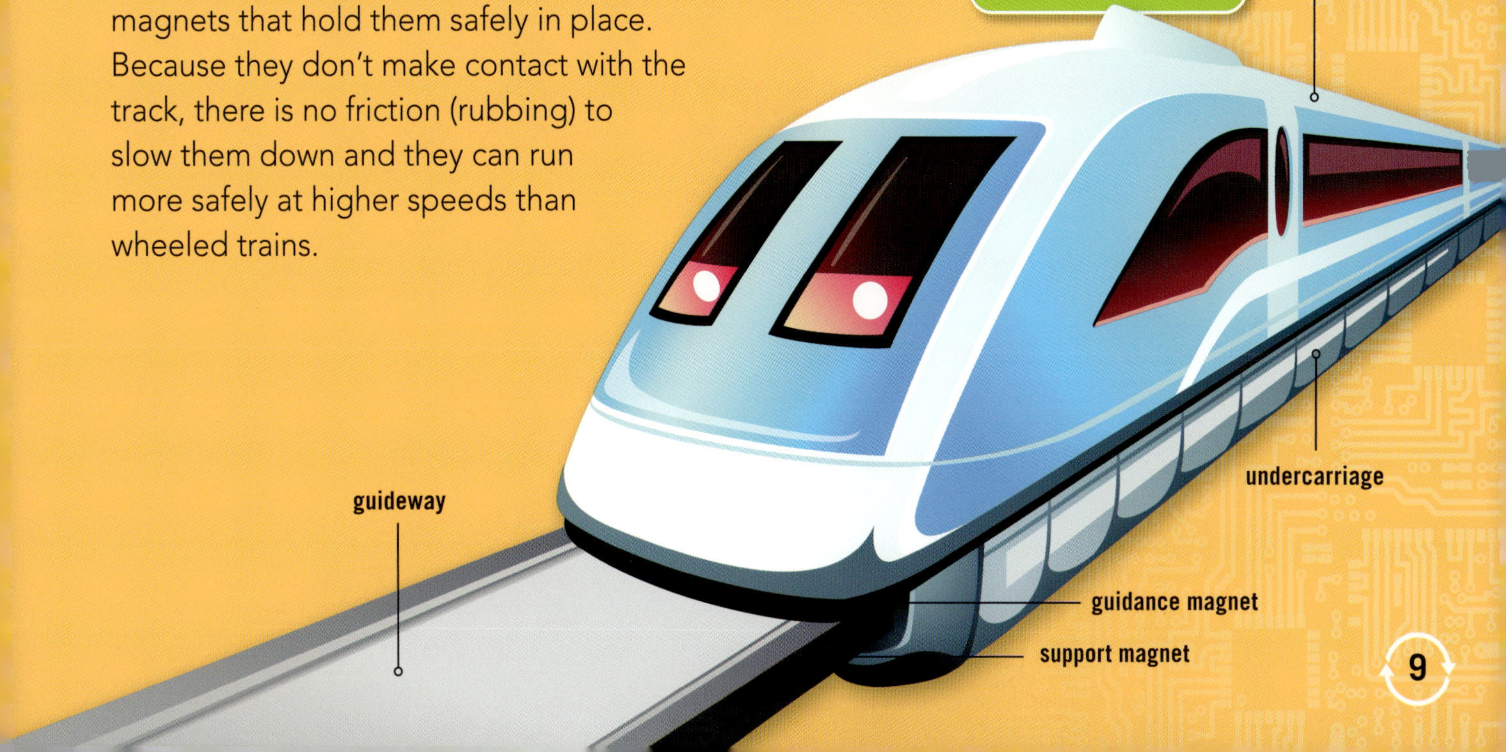

a maglev train

WIND POWER

Have you ever felt the wind pushing so hard against you that you can barely walk through it? Wind—that is, moving air—is an invisible but powerful force! We can capture the energy of the wind's movement, which we call its "kinetic energy," and turn it into clean, green electricity.

INSIDE A WIND TURBINE

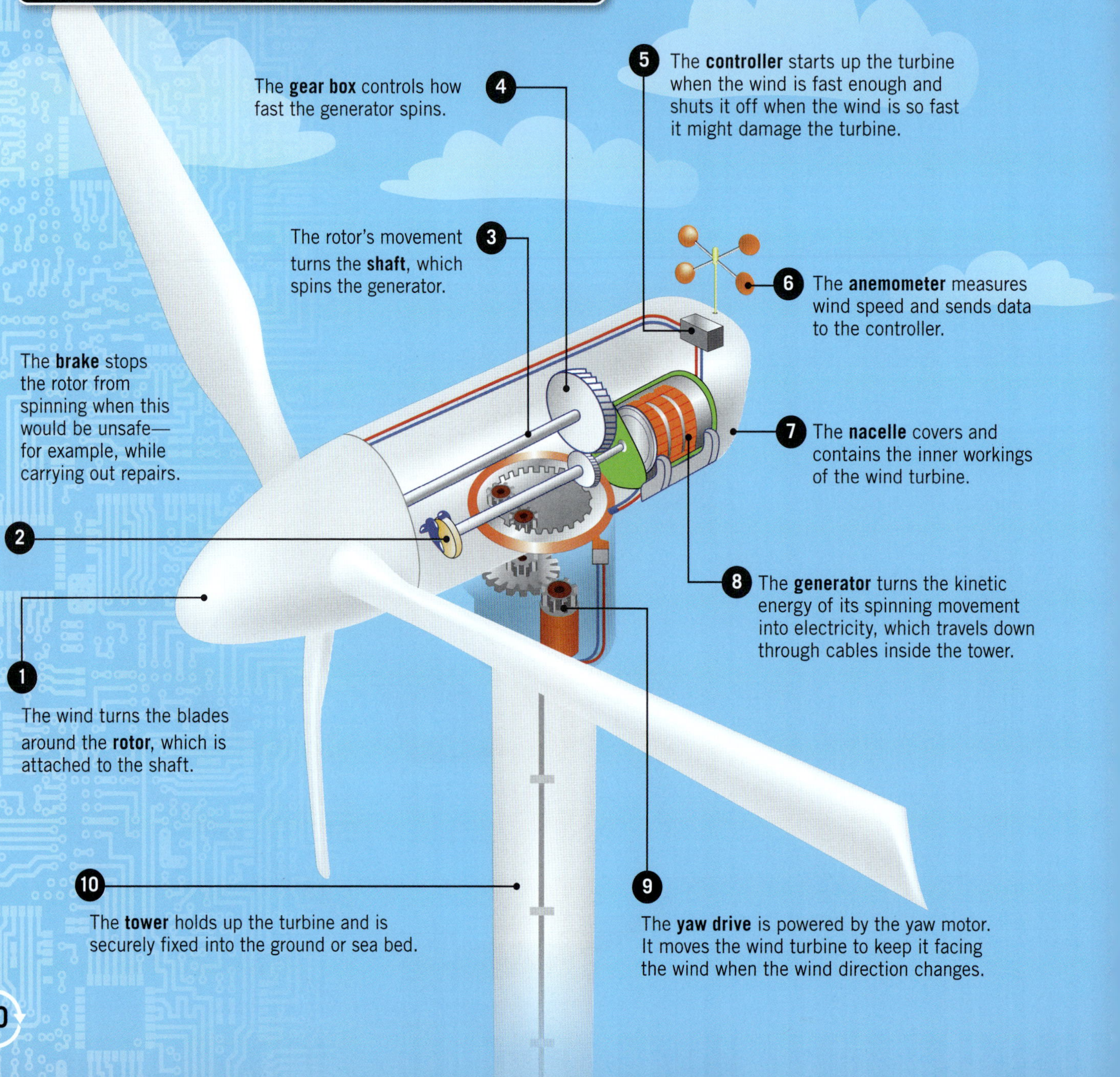

WIND FARMS

Wind farms are groups of turbines placed together on land (onshore) or at sea (offshore). Offshore wind turbines are fixed to the sea bed with tall, roughly cylinder-shaped foundations made of steel or concrete. These foundations raise them high above the waves. The tower, nacelle, and rotor are brought out separately on boats and lifted into place by cranes.

Although wind farms ultimately help wildlife by reducing the threat of climate change, they can hurt and disturb wild birds, so it's important to build them away from areas in which lots of birds live or travel.

SUPPLY AND STORAGE

Electricity from wind turbine generators travels along cables via substations that change its voltage to make it energy-efficient and safe to use in buildings. It sometimes goes to electricity storage plants, where it is stored in batteries to give us a more constant, reliable power supply.

DID YOU KNOW?

Wind and solar power (see pages 12–13) still only produce 7 percent of global electricity, despite being its cheapest sources. Governments can change this by supporting these green technologies instead of paying fossil fuel companies to keep their prices low.

SOLAR POWER

The sun is a clean, green energy source that we can use to charge up our phones, heat water for a nice shower, or even power a spacecraft!

SOLAR CELLS

Solar, or photovoltaic, cells capture sunlight's energy and turn it into electricity. Multiple cells are arranged into solar panels, which are used individually or grouped together in solar farms to generate more power. Let's take a look inside a cell…

Calculators are often powered by solar cells.

1. A solar cell is made of a super-thin layer of silicon, which has been heated up in a special way and surrounded by two metal sheets—solid underneath and mesh on top.

2. When tiny particles of sunlight called photons hit the silicon layer, they travel down and transfer their energy to other tiny particles called electrons inside it. These electrons are held inside larger, but still very small, particles called atoms.

3. The electrons "jump" away from their atoms and flow around the circuit as electricity until they reunite with another atom on the other side of the solar cell. This flow of electrons is an electric current.

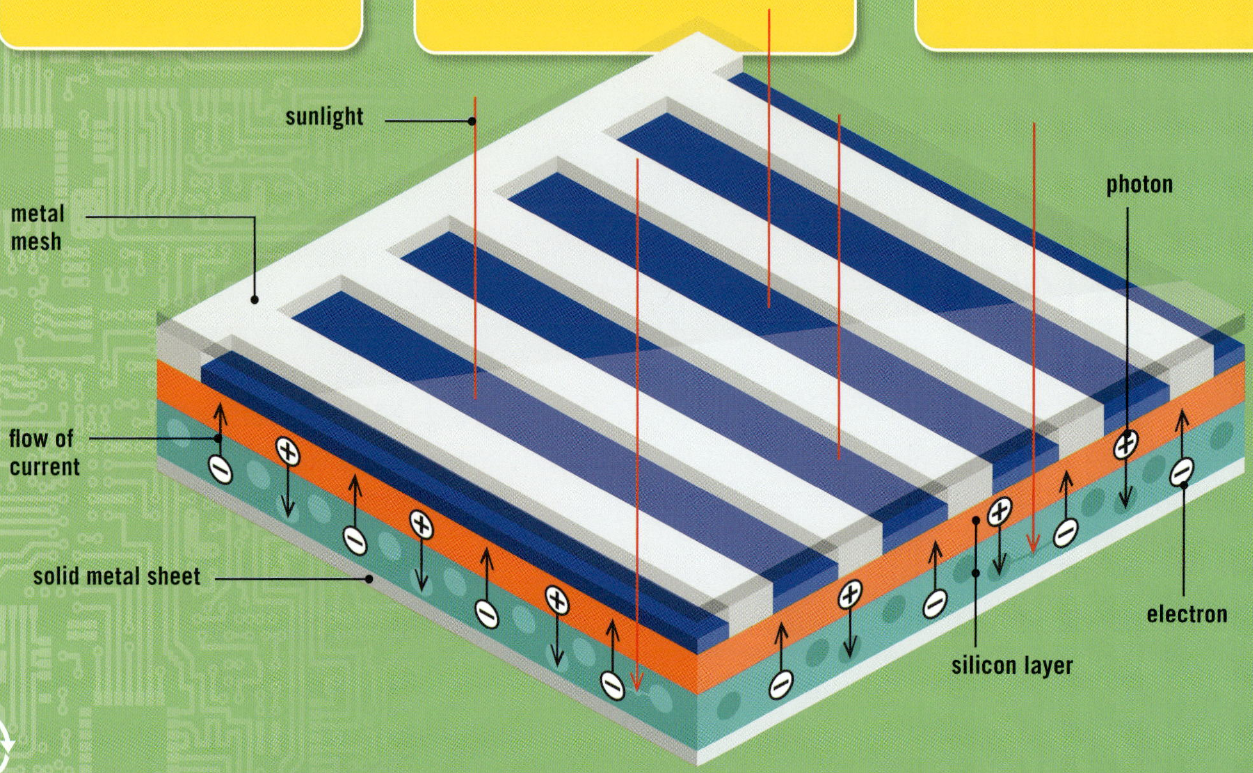

SOLAR HEATING SYSTEM

We use a different type of solar panel to collect the sun's heat energy. People install these panels—called "collectors"—on their roofs to heat their home and water supply. A fluid is pumped up and through the collector, where it warms up if the day is sunny. Then it travels back down to heat a water storage tank, which sends hot water along pipes to radiators, taps, and so on.

From lab to reality

- **Invention of first photovoltaic cell:** Announced in 1954 by Bell Labs in the US
- **Change in average solar cell cost, 1977–2020:** From $76.67 to 16 cents per watt (a watt is the unit we use to measure power)

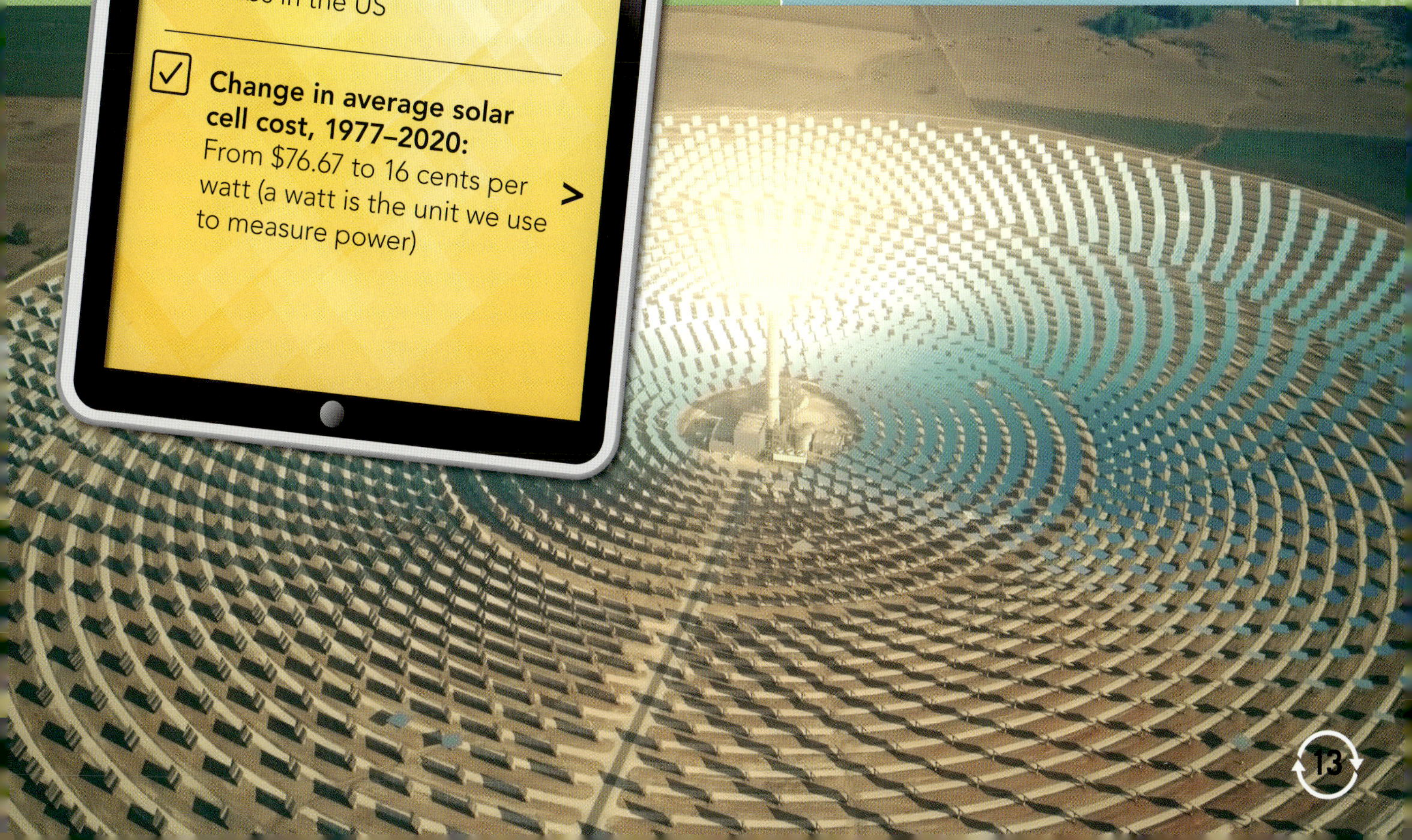

Solar thermal power plants, like this one in southern Spain, use mirrors to direct sunlight onto receivers that capture the sun's heat. This heat is used to create steam that spins generators, producing electricity.

GEOTHERMAL ENERGY AND GROUND SOURCE HEAT

Earth's center is hot, hot, hot! Heat from our planet's core travels up and out toward the surface, warming underground rocks, water, and gas along the way. We can capture this clean, green energy to heat our homes and generate electricity in power plants.

GROUND SOURCE HEAT PUMP SYSTEM

This home-based system typically works by pumping cold water down through a loop of pipes just below Earth's surface, where the temperature stays at a steady 50-60°F (10-16°C). The water gets nice and warm as it travels through the underground pipes, then travels back up to heat the house and its water supply.

Some ground source heat pumps can reverse direction in hot weather, so water that is warmer than 50-60°F (10-16°C) is cooled underground and then used to cool the house.

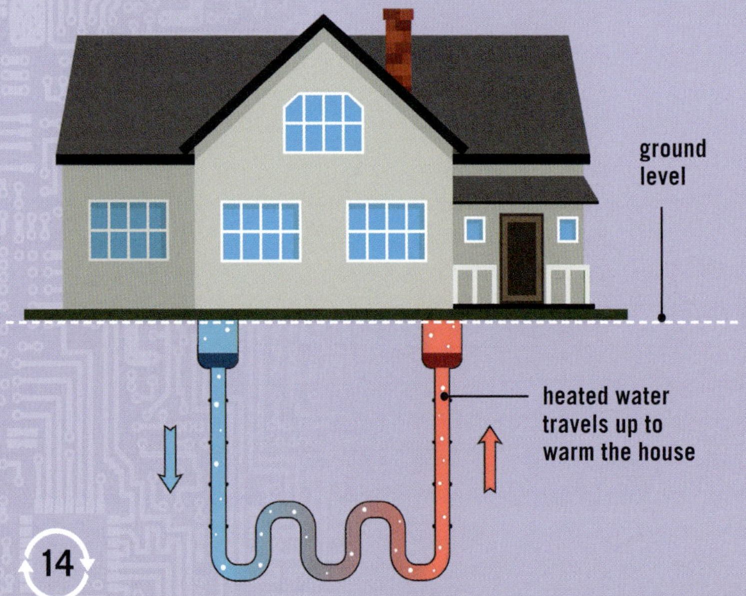

GEOTHERMAL POWER PLANTS

In some parts of the world, such as Indonesia and Iceland, it gets particularly hot relatively close to the Earth's surface. This means there are often lots of hot springs, geysers, and active volcanoes. This makes these places perfect for geothermal power plants. One plant can typically power thousands of homes, although the exact number depends on the plant's size and how much energy locals use.

Geysers release jets of hot water and steam through holes in Earth's surface.

DID YOU KNOW?

The center of Earth may be as hot as the surface of the sun—around 10,830°F (6,000°C)!

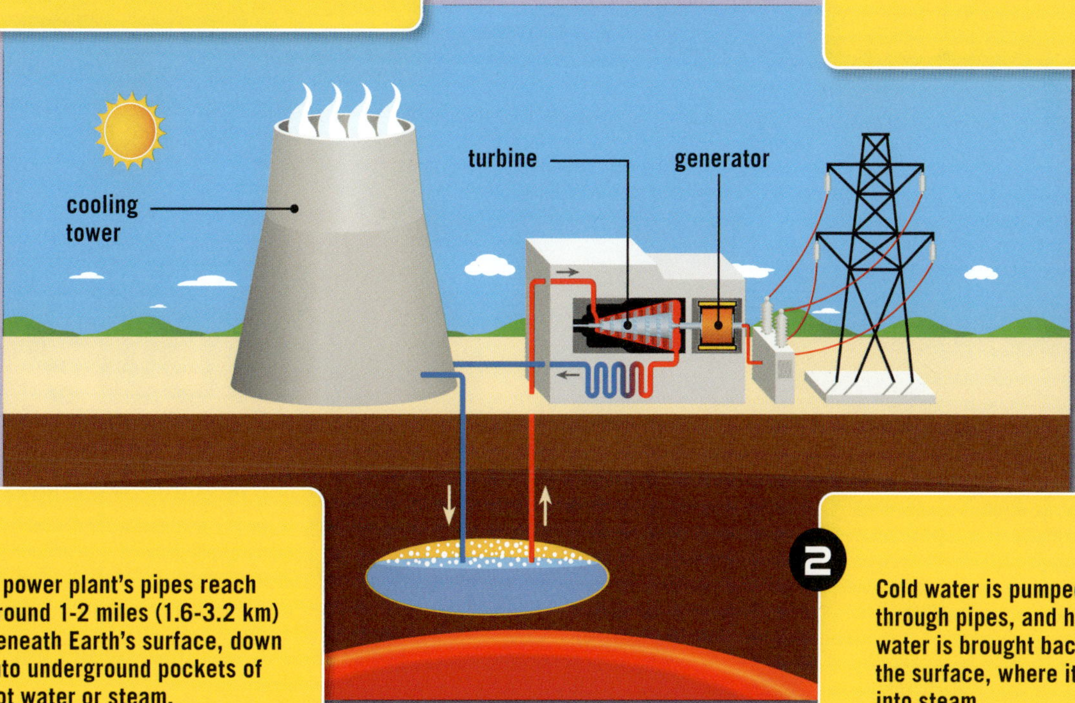

1 A power plant's pipes reach around 1-2 miles (1.6-3.2 km) beneath Earth's surface, down into underground pockets of hot water or steam.

2 Cold water is pumped down through pipes, and heated water is brought back up to the surface, where it turns into steam.

3 This steam spins a turbine, and a connected generator produces electricity from the kinetic (moving) energy.

4 The steam then passes into a cooling tower, where it turns back into cold water to be pumped underground again.

USING SATELLITES

One often-overlooked area of green technology is the range of tools that scientists use to collect evidence of climate change. Data from satellites can show how global warming is affecting Earth, helping us predict future climate patterns and try to prevent—or at least prepare for—these changes.

Satellite stats

- **First artificial satellite:** Sputnik I, launched in 1957
- **Number of working satellites orbiting Earth in 2019:** Around 2,000
- **Satellite orbit speed:** Depends on how far it is from Earth; for most satellites tracking climate change, around 1.5-5 miles (2-8 km) per second

A satellite is a device sent into space to orbit Earth, collecting information or acting as part of a communication system.

DID YOU KNOW?

Old, worn-out satellites are removed from Earth's orbit so they don't crash into active satellites. They are blasted further out into space or slowed down until they fall and burn up in Earth's atmosphere.

PLANET PHOTOSHOOT

Satellites can take large-scale photographs of Earth's surface, showing where and how quickly forest fires are spreading or areas of ice are shrinking as they melt. Scientists compare pictures taken over the years to track changes and patterns.

The devastating 2019-20 Australian bushfires, which burned over 20 percent of the country's forests, were visible from space.

WORKING WITH WAVES

Satellites can be specially designed to detect all sorts of invisible waves. Some use sensors to measure how much heat gas particles in Earth's atmosphere are giving off, then analyze this data to work out the air temperature. Others track levels of greenhouse gases in the atmosphere by shining out lasers to measure different gases' wavelengths.

MAKING MAPS

Some satellites send out waves, too; they bounce off Earth and back to the satellites, where sensors pick them up. This technology can be used to create maps of Earth's surface that give us information about sea levels, soil moisture levels, and more. Scientists often confirm their evidence by comparing satellites' findings with measurements taken on Earth's surface.

EXTRACTING ICE CORES

Earth has all kinds of natural records that can tell us what its climate and atmosphere were like far into the past. Scientists study records such as corals, rocks, the rings of tree trunks, and the layers of ice cores—long cylinders of ice drawn out from deep within ice sheets and glaciers in different parts of the world.

Rings of tree trunks can tell us about the climate in the past.

An ice core extracted by a powered drill.

DRILLING DOWN

Scientists extract ice cores using a long drill with a hole down the middle. The drill cuts or melts away a ring of ice as it travels down, filling the hole inside with a cylinder of ice that is then brought up to the surface.

Scientists are now able to extract ice cores that are hundreds of thousands, or even millions, of years old. As the ice is built up year on year by thin layers of fallen snow, it gets older and older the further you dig beneath its top surface.

DIFFERENT DRILLS

Scientists use a hand-operated drill called a hand auger to extract ice cores from fairly close to the surface. If they want to dig deeper, they use a powered drill that can reach down hundreds or thousands of feet. This type of drill is much bigger and requires an energy source, such as solar panels or fuel-powered generators.

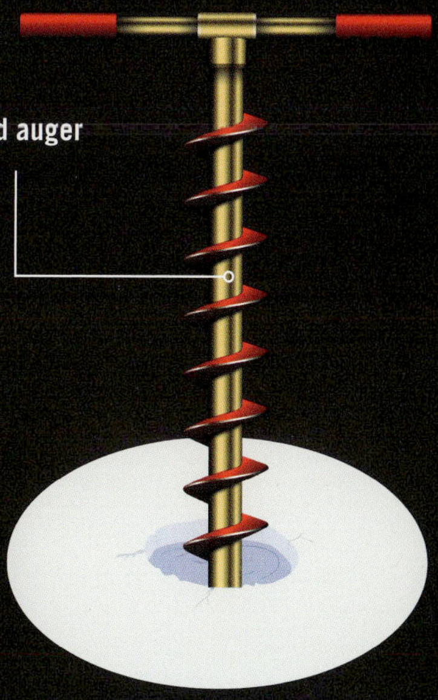

LEARNING FROM THE PAST

By studying ice core layers and the gas bubbles and solid particles trapped in them, scientists can better understand how changing amounts of greenhouse gases in Earth's atmosphere may affect its temperature and long-term weather patterns.

They can use this data in computer simulations to help them predict, for example, how much and how quickly current carbon dioxide levels might raise Earth's temperature.

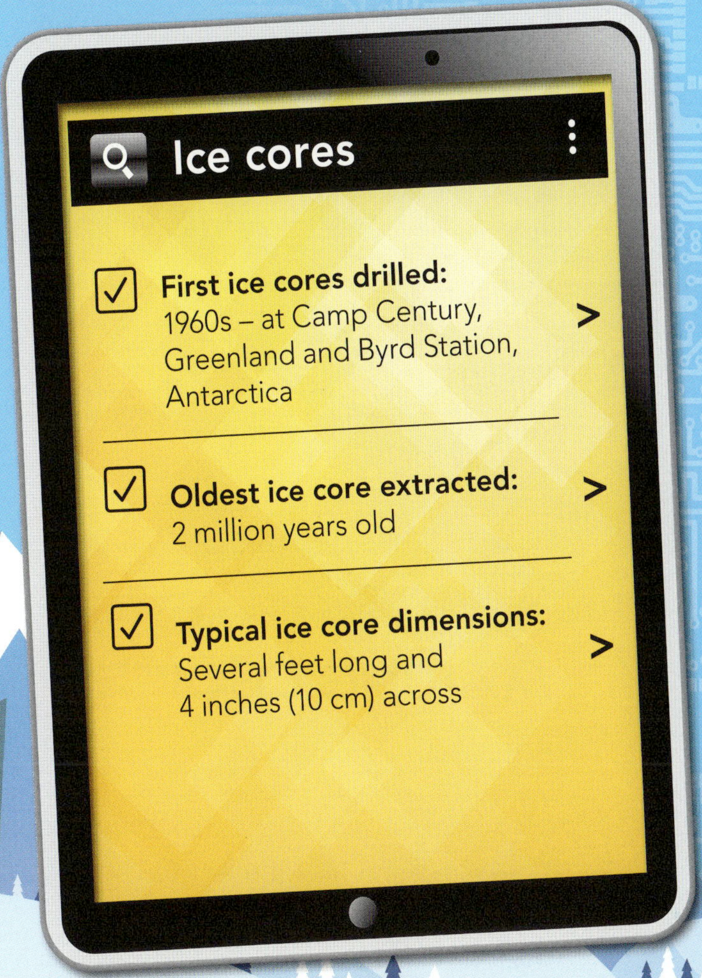

LAB-GROWN MEAT

Our planet just can't sustain the amount of meat—especially beef—that we're currently eating, and it is one of the major contributors to climate change. Producing beef creates 20 times more emissions than plant-based protein sources, such as beans and lentils. One major reason for this is that cow farts and burps release lots of methane, a greenhouse gas.

Huge areas of forest, including tropical rainforests home to rare and endangered plants and animals, are cut down or burned every day to make room for cows to graze. This releases lots of carbon dioxide, a greenhouse gas, into Earth's atmosphere.

MAKING CHOICES

Many people choose to reduce the amount of meat they eat, to opt for less environmentally damaging meats such as chicken, or to give up meat altogether. However, for those people who just can't imagine going without their steaks and burgers, technology may be able to help!

FROM TEST TUBE TO TABLE

The first lab-grown burger was cooked and eaten in London, UK, in 2013. The basic steps taken to create it were:

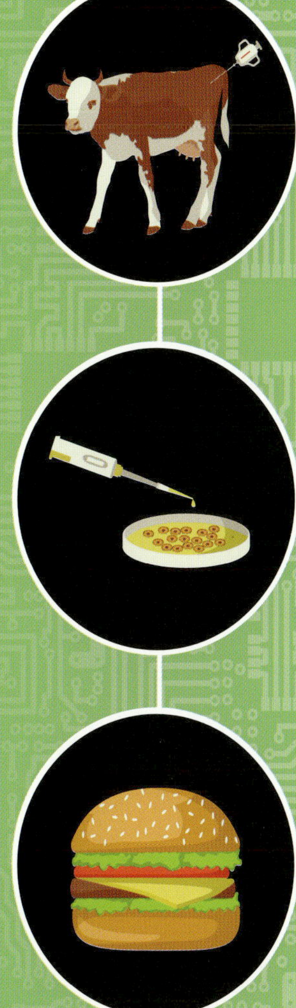

1. **Take stem cells (which can develop into different types of body tissue) from a single live animal.**
2. **Bathe the cells in a nutrient- and chemical-packed liquid to help them develop and multiply. The cells eventually form strips of muscle.**
3. **Process these meat strips into small pellets, which are squished together to form a burger. Add beetroot juice to stain the white meat a more beef-like color.**

Teams of scientists around the world are now trying to make "cultured meat" available on a large scale. They are developing a variety of methods to make it as tasty, safe, healthy, eco-friendly, and affordable as possible.

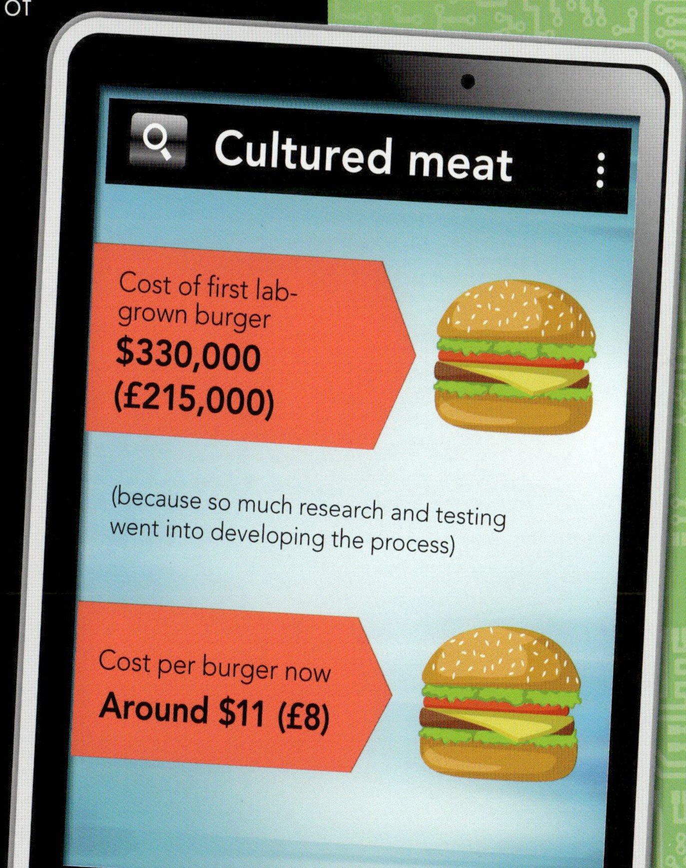

DID YOU KNOW?

Some experts think cultured meat could be safer and healthier to eat than traditional meat. Meat from farmed animals can carry diseases and pollution, and cultured meat can be made with healthier forms of fat.

CLIMATE-RESISTANT CROPS

Climate change causes unpredictable weather, which can make growing crops difficult. If the temperature or rainfall is different than expected at certain times of the year, plants may die or not grow well. However, what if we could specially breed plants to survive and thrive in changing conditions?

Droughts often cause crops to fail, but climate-resistant crops could manage better in hot, dry soil.

SELECTIVE BREEDING

When plants reproduce, they pass on their genes to their plant offspring. Genes give living things instructions for how they should develop—for example, a sunflower's genes tell it to grow tall and produce a big, flat, yellow flower.

We can selectively breed together plants with helpful traits so their offspring are more likely to have these traits too. A plant may grow better in hot, dry conditions if it is selectively bred from plants that have longer roots (to search out water) and wider leaves (to cover more of the surrounding soil and stop it from losing moisture).

GENETIC MODIFICATION (GM)

Scientists can also genetically modify plants to help them adapt to climate change, or knock-on effects such as more diseases and pests. They insert genes (see page 22) from one plant into the cells of a second plant – sometimes one that isn't of the same species. When the second plant reproduces, it passes along these genes with its original ones. There is no evidence that eating GM foods is dangerous, but there are some concerns about how GM crops might affect wild plants and animals.

GM crops

- ✓ **First GM crop created:** Antibiotic-resistant tobacco plant, 1983 >
- ✓ **First GM food approved:** Flavr Savr tomato, USA, 1994 >
- ✓ **First GM soybean crop sold: 1996. 94 percent of the USA's soybean crops are now genetically modified** >

NOT GIVING UP

Taking steps to adapt to climate change, such as breeding climate-resistant crops, doesn't mean we're "giving up." Solving the climate crisis should always remain the goal, but we also need to take care of people already suffering its effects – for example, those in low-income countries who may starve if their crops fail.

SOLAR GEOENGINEERING

Geoengineering is what we call attempts to slow or stop climate change by manipulating Earth's natural systems on a large scale. For instance, solar geoengineering aims to cool down Earth by reflecting more sunlight away from it and back out into space.

Large, white areas of ice on Earth's surface, which naturally reflect back sunlight, are shrinking due to climate change.

A BIG GAMBLE

A number of solar geoengineering ideas are currently being developed, and lots of people are excited about the possibility of finding fast-acting solutions to climate change.

But Earth's natural systems are complex, and many scientists are wary of relying on extreme, untested ideas rather than focusing on cutting emissions. They worry that solar geoengineering could not work at all, or could end up causing very serious, unexpected problems.

DID YOU KNOW?

In the last 50 years or so, Greenland's ice sheet has lost enough water to fill around 16 trillion (16,000,000,000,000) bathtubs.

REFLECTING SUNLIGHT

Here are some solar geoengineering ideas for how to make Earth's surface more reflective so that it will bounce more sunlight back into space, cooling the planet:

1. **Use more white or mirrored materials for the roofs of buildings, and light-colored materials for roads.**

2. **Plant varieties of common crops, such as maize, with more light-reflecting features – for example, a waxier coating on their leaves.**

3. **Create lots of tiny air bubbles in the sea so the light hits them, rather than being absorbed by the dark water.**

4. **Use ships to spray sea salt into the atmosphere so water droplets form around the particles, creating more reflective clouds.**

5. **Launch solar reflectors – essentially giant mirrors – into orbit around Earth, to bounce away sunlight before it hits Earth's surface or its lower atmosphere.**

How solar reflectors might look as they orbit Earth.

CARBON CAPTURE AND STORAGE

Carbon capture is another type of geoengineering, which aims to suck carbon dioxide out of Earth's atmosphere. The idea is that with less carbon dioxide to trap the Sun's heat, global warming will be slowed or stopped. This carbon dioxide needs to be stored securely underground, deep in the ocean, or within certain types of rocks to stop it escaping.

ARTIFICIAL TREES

Trees naturally take in carbon dioxide from the air, so why design artificial ones to do the same job? Fans of this technology claim artificial trees could capture carbon much quicker and more efficiently than real ones, and could be installed in spots where the soil is too shallow for tree roots.

Critics point out that artificial trees are very expensive (one estimate is $353,000 [£270,000] per tree), that they don't support plant and animal life like real trees can, and that it's unclear how practical and effective they might be on a large scale.

Artificial trees typically have parts coated with a special liquid that absorbs carbon dioxide.

BIOENERGY WITH CARBON CAPTURE AND STORAGE (BECCS)

BECCS is a way of producing energy by burning plants, and collecting and storing the carbon dioxide released. Because plants take in carbon dioxide as they grow, the idea is that BECCS could reduce carbon dioxide in the atmosphere. However, some scientists worry that BECCS might not work well enough on a large scale to live up to its hype.

There are also concerns that governments and businesses might see it as a "magic fix," helping them to meet carbon-cutting targets without actually reducing emissions elsewhere. Another issue is that growing plants for bioenergy takes away land for food crops, and may mean lots of trees are cut down to make more space.

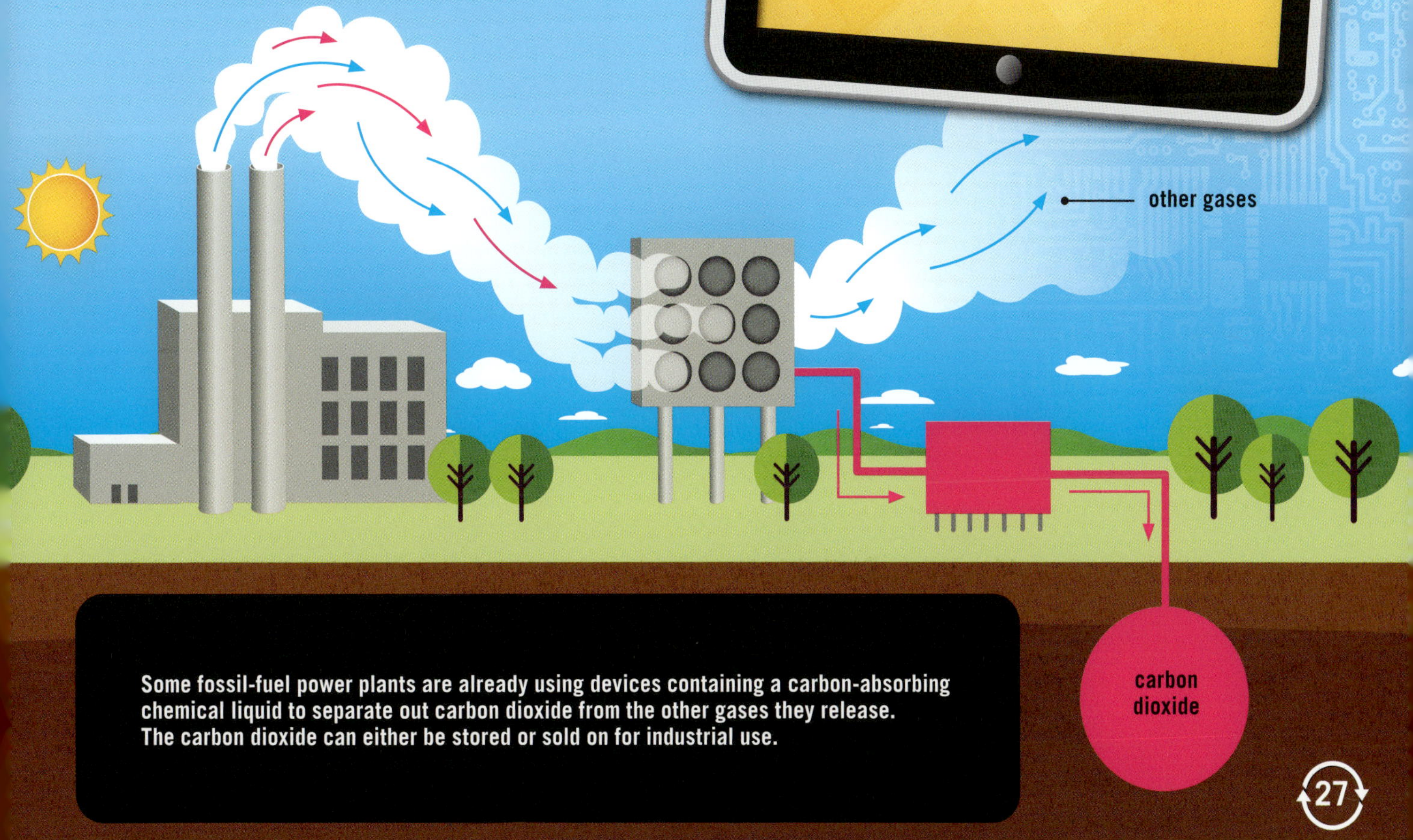

Some fossil-fuel power plants are already using devices containing a carbon-absorbing chemical liquid to separate out carbon dioxide from the other gases they release. The carbon dioxide can either be stored or sold on for industrial use.

REFORESTATION AND REWILDING

Shiny, new hi-tech solutions can be really exciting, but sometimes the best and most reliable technologies are the ones Earth provides naturally – and for free! Healthy forests, wetlands, oceans and soils remove huge amounts of carbon dioxide from Earth's atmosphere.

Humans have destroyed lots of these habitats but all isn't lost – we can work to restore them. It can take a long time – decades or longer – to get back the same carbon-capture benefits, though, so it's really important to protect the wild areas we still have.

REFORESTATION

Reforesting means planting trees where forests have been cut down. It is one of the best ways to solve the climate crisis – if we do it right.

That means, for example, choosing trees that won't suck up lots of groundwater and leave the land too dry, and leaving gaps between areas of trees to stop fires spreading. If we don't plant smart, all the new trees could die off – or burn in forest fires, releasing more carbon dioxide.

REWILDING

Nature has all sorts of complicated, overlapping systems and it often seems to know better than we do how best to repair itself.

But when humans have seriously upset habitats' natural balance, we may need to give a few helpful nudges to get things going, before leaving nature alone to do the rest. This is called rewilding, and it often involves reintroducing plants and animals into habitats where they are an important part of healthy natural systems.

DID YOU KNOW?

Huge underground networks of thread-like fungi help trees and other forest plants "talk" to one another, sharing warnings about pests, weather and more.

Destroying and planting trees

- ☑ **Amount of Earth's forests cut down every year:** An area the size of the UK
- ☑ **Tree-planting world record:** 50 million trees in one year (2016), by around 800,000 people in India

GLOSSARY

anemometer the part of a wind turbine that measures wind speed

atmosphere the layers of gases surrounding a planet or other object in space

climate long-term weather conditions and temperature patterns

data information, facts and figures collected and used to better understand something

drought long period with little or no rain, leading to water shortages

emissions substances – typically harmful, polluting gases – released into the air

fossil fuel natural fuel, such as oil, that takes millions of years to form and can be burned for energy or heat

generator machine that turns energy from movement into electricity

greenhouse gas gas that traps the Sun's heat in Earth's atmosphere, warming our planet

kinetic energy the energy that something (e.g. the wind) has because of its movement

mesh material made of lots of different strands of wire, plastic or thread woven together, with spaces between them

nacelle the part of a wind turbine that covers its inner machinery

orbit to circle around and around a planet, star or other object in space

particle tiny object or piece of something

rotor the part of a wind turbine around which the blades move

silicon natural material that is often used in electronic devices

trench long, narrow pit dug into the ground

turbine machine that generates power by using a gas or liquid to turn moving parts

yaw drive the part of a wind turbine that moves it around to face the wind direction

FURTHER INFORMATION

BOOKS

This Book Will (Help) Cool the Climate
by Isabel Thomas (Wren & Rook)

Discover 50 practical ways that you can help to stop climate change and protect our planet.

Eco STEAM: The Energy We Use
by Georgia Amson-Bradshaw (Wayland)

Find out how we generate and use energy, and how we can best meet our energy needs while caring for Earth.

What is Climate Change?
by Louise Spilsbury (Wayland)

Learn more about what is causing climate change and how we can work together to stop it.

VIDEOS

Crash Course Kids: Engineering
youtu.be/owHF9iLyxic

What exactly does an engineer do? This video explains how engineers can design technologies to help solve all kinds of problems, even ones as big as climate change.

I'm Only a Kid, I Can't Do Anything about Climate Change... Right?
youtu.be/PslL9WC-2cQ

Discover how kids and young people just like you can help to stop climate change.

Climate Change: Earth's Giant Game of Tetris
youtu.be/ztWHqUFJRTs

What does the video game Tetris have to do with climate change? Find out in this video!

INDEX

animals **11, 20, 21, 23, 26, 29**

atmosphere **4, 16, 17, 18, 19, 25, 26, 27, 28**

business **5, 11, 27**

carbon dioxide **4, 19, 26–27, 28**

costs **6, 7, 8, 11, 13, 21, 26**

diseases **21, 23**

electricity **6, 7, 8, 10, 11, 12, 13, 14, 15**

emissions **5, 6, 7, 20, 24, 27**

energy **7, 10–11, 12–13, 14–15, 19, 27**

fires **5, 17, 28**

food **20–21, 22–23, 27**

forests **4, 5, 17, 20, 28, 29**

fuel **4, 6, 7, 9, 11, 19, 27**

genetic modification (GM) **23**

geoengineering **24–25, 26**

global warming **4, 16, 26**

government **5, 8, 11, 27**

greenhouse gases **4–5, 6, 17, 19, 20**

homes **13, 14, 15**

ice **17, 18–19, 24**

ocean **9, 11, 17, 25, 26, 28**

plants **20, 22–23, 25, 26, 27, 29**

pollution **6, 7, 8, 9, 21**

power plants **7, 13, 14, 15, 27**

rain **5, 22**

soil **17, 22, 26, 28**

sunlight **4, 12–13, 24–25, 26**

temperature **5, 14, 17, 19, 22**

transport **6–7, 8–9**

weather **5, 14, 19, 22, 29**